SEX
FOR LAZY
PEOPLE

SEX
FOR LAZY
PEOPLE

50 Effortless Positions
So You Can Do It Without Overdoing It

GINNY HOGAN
Illustrated by Iván Bravo

CHRONICLE BOOKS
SAN FRANCISCO

Library of Congress Cataloging-in-Publication Data

Names: Hogan, Ginny, author. |
Bravo, Iván, illustrator.
Title: Sex for lazy people : 50 effortless positions
so you can do it without overdoing it /
Ginny Hogan ; illustrated by Iván Bravo.
Description: San Francisco : Chronicle Books, [2023]
Identifiers: LCCN 2023007066 |
ISBN 9781797225012 (paperback)
Subjects: LCSH: Sexual intercours--Humor. |
Sex instruction--Humor.
Classification: LCC HQ31 .H65 2023 |
DDC 306.7702/07--dc23/eng/20230314
LC record available at https://lccn.loc.gov/2023007066

Manufactured in India.

MIX
Paper | Supporting
responsible forestry
FSC™ C016779

Design by Maggie Edelman.

Illustrations by Iván Bravo.

MTA is a registered trademark of MTA
Distributors, LLC. Postmates is a registered trademark of Uber
Technologies, INC.

10 9 8 7 6 5 4 3 2 1

Chronicle Books LLC
680 Second Street
San Francisco, CA 94107
www.chroniclebooks.com

INTRODUCTION

If you've been described as "sexually active," you may be trying too hard. There's no need to be active in the bedroom. Just look at the language—you're getting laid. Passive voice. You're not laying.

Sex is fun, but it has one major downside—it takes work. As such, it can be hard to find the energy. Maybe you've had a long day at work, you need to cook dinner, your kids are crying, and you're exhausted. Or maybe you don't have a job, you order Postmates every night, and you're childless—but you're exhausted nonetheless and need your good eight, or twenty, hours of sleep every night or else. People don't need a reason to be tired, and they definitely don't need a reason to be lazy. So if you're in that boat, this book is for you. Here you'll find sex positions that require minimal effort, and tips to keep it that way.

The idea that sex needs to be onerous is a misconception. Sex is almost meant to be lazy—it often happens between two people, and people are inherently lazy, which means that two people are twice as lazy (imagine how much laziness there is at an orgy!). In this book we'll give you some ideas for how to keep sex fun, simple, and—most importantly—effortless. We offer some unexciting positions you can try any time, day or night (just as long as it's not during the eight or twenty hours you're asleep, or your very justified two-hour nap). Try your hand at the Sliding into Home Plate, in which you turn your apartment into a lubricated fun house to avoid having to walk to the bedroom, or learn more about the Stop, Drop, and Roll, where you do just that—emphasis on the "stopping." Speaking of which, let's all stop striving so hard. There's no reason to exhaust yourself for it, because sex can be fun without engaging in a full-blown cardio workout.

So if you're looking for some inspiration on how to go forth and get laid lazily, we've got you covered. And don't worry about getting through all the positions today . . . or tomorrow . . . or this year . . . or this lifetime. The point, after all, is to be lazy. So read on, and never wear yourself out.

The Rotating Kebab

One of the most exhausting parts of sex can be constantly switching positions, but sometimes it has to happen. We recommend starting in missionary, then rotating your position ninety degrees. Continue periodically until you are back in missionary. That way, you get four total switches with minimal effort.

The Melatonin

Let's say you and your partner both find that having an orgasm right before bed is a great way to ensure you sleep through the night. Let's also say you're both exhausted and want to finish as quickly as possible. Lie in bed and get each other off. And then, if you also want some real melatonin, go ahead.

The Beanbag Chair

Not only are beanbag chairs super cool, but they're also prime for lazing. Get two beanbag chairs and angle them so that you can reach each other. Then, enjoy a relaxing sit while getting each other off.

The Spoon

Be the little spoon for your partner, while also
licking a spoonful of ice cream. Or try being
the big spoon, if you think you can do it without
getting ice cream in their hair.

The Reverse Turtle-girl

This one is a low-energy substitute for the reverse cowgirl, because even a cow is way too active. One person lies on their back and the other is on top facing away. This way, both people are in a resting position, and there's no eye contact, hence no pressure to do something sexy with your face. Move slowly—slow and steady wins the race, after all.

JUST THE TIPS

- **Have sex with someone hot. This makes the whole thing easier.**

- **Keep a box of tissues on your nightstand for easy cleanup. I mean, everyone knows this.**

- **Use a condom. Putting it on kills time in the beginning, which you can count toward your total amount of time spent laboring. Plus, it makes cleanup a lot easier!**
  NOTE: If neither party present at the sex has a penis, put one on a banana so you can still kill some time.

The Exercise Ball

Have seated sex on an exercise ball. The person on the bottom can firmly plant their feet on the ground and use the ball's natural bounciness to do some of the heavy lifting.

The Butterfly

Put your feet together and open your knees out to the side, preparing for a butterfly stretch. Lean forward until you feel a pleasant pull on your groin—further, yeah, further. Ohhhh yeah. Your partner is there for moral support, but if you do it with no pants on, you might give them a bit of a show.

JUST THE TIP!

Wear very loose-fitting clothing! It's easier to stretch in, and it's easier to take off.

The Suds

Take turns spraying the other's genitals with the showerhead. This allows each person to feel like they're getting their partner off without actually using any part of their body.

JUST THE TIP!

Shower sex may seem to require more effort because one of you might have to bend your knees and keep your feet from slipping, but keep in mind that it's a two-for-one activity. Make sure you wash your hair when you're in there so you don't have to make a second trip.

The Benchwarmer

Only so many people can fit on even the largest of beds, so if your orgy is big enough, you'll get tagged out at some point. The more people you invite, the longer you get to hang on the bench.

JUST THE TIPS

- If you're single and looking to get it on (lazily, within reason), but your apartment is dirty, invite someone over for sex who has successfully given you head in the past. It's the only motivator strong enough to make you pull out the vacuum cleaner.

- Keep a protein bar on your nightstand in case the sex ends up getting more labor-intensive than you had planned and you need to stop for a snack.

The Break Room

If you work from home and skip an important meeting to have sex, it's lazy no matter what position you're in because you blew off your job to be there. Good work!

JUST THE TIP!

Get an ergonomic chair with a wide seat that supports your back and allows you to keep your legs splayed open. This way, you can shift comfortably from work to sex without adjusting your legs.

The Rom-Com

Have breathless, wild sex for seven seconds, cum, then dramatically fall asleep.

Doggie Style

Check your assumptions—this is where your partner dutifully sleeps at the foot of the bed.

JUST THE TIP!

Turn your phone off during sex. Leaving it on may prompt a question about why you checked your phone during sex, which requires more attention and thought than you want to expend, and could lead to a very exhausting fight. Although, if you really want to leave your phone on, that might work too, because your mom might call you, which could put an end to the sex.

The "Kids Are Sleeping"

Decide ahead of time that you're not going to make any noise. Note that this applies whether or not you have kids—somebody's kids are always sleeping somewhere.

JUST THE TIP!

Stuffy neighbors also work! They provide a foolproof excuse for why you need to keep the sex volume down. Quiet sex is far less energy-intensive, with lower expectations. Do you know how creepy it is to be completely wild, but silent? Don't do that.

Sliding into Home Plate

Hire someone to lube your entire apartment. That way, when you walk through the door, you will seamlessly glide into your partner.

JUST THE TIP!

Unfortunately, it's best practice to pee right after sex. This is very hard for lazy people, as it involves standing up and walking—obviously too much work. To minimize discomfort, make sure the slip includes a slide to the bathroom.

The Role-Play

Role-play can be a really creative way to spice up your sex life while maintaining laziness—if you choose your roles correctly. The characters of "doctor who is exhausted from a long day of surgery" and "nurse who is exhausted from a long day of surgery" are recommended. This way, you don't have to worry about making excuses.

JUST THE TIP!

If you don't have the time—or energy—to figure out role-appropriate dirty talk, try rehearsing ahead of time so that regurgitating it later is simply a matter of muscle memory. It's easier if you pick one phrase to say over and over again. Some suggestions include "Cum for me," "Can't wait for you to cum," and "Paging Dr. Cum to cum over here and cum."

JUST THE TIPS

- Keep note of what times of day you and your partner feel most energized. Then, pick the intervals that overlap. This may only be between 1:06 p.m. and 1:08 p.m., so be prepared to do it quickly.

- Leave your legs open at all times, as wide as is comfortable, to ensure your partner's easy access. This cuts down on "getting into position" time for both of you.

Stop, Drop, and Roll

Stop what you're doing, drop to the ground wherever you are, and roll to your partner to have sex on the floor. This way, you don't need to do the laborious work of walking to the bedroom.

The Skateboard

Having sex on a skateboard might not seem lazy, but it can be. Lay on it and plant your feet on the ground with your partner doing the same on a different skateboard. This way you can rock into each other without the hard work of thrusting.

The French Press

Chug a ton of coffee before sex so your energy returns to you in the middle of the act.

JUST THE TIP!

Schedule your sex so you know ahead of time how much to caffeinate.

The Fire Alarm

Leave something in the oven and wait until the fire alarm has gone off to start having sex. This ensures you wrap things up quickly—sex is great and all, but it's better when it's short.

JUST THE TIP!

If you don't want to commit arson if things accidentally get out of hand (or the sex is, like, really good), skip creating a fire hazard and find a time-sensitive alternative, like ordering Postmates before you begin foreplay so it arrives just as you're finishing.

The Bed, Bath, and Beyond

One of you lies on your back. The other lies on top. Do whatever you want, it doesn't matter—either way, one of you has a comfy mattress topper and the other has a weighted blanket, both of which you've been too lazy to buy. It's a win-win scenario.

JUST THE TIP!

To avoid ever having to wash your sheets, simply get another bed and designate it only for sex. Let it get as dirty as you like because you're not sleeping there anyway.

The MTA

Have sex for thirty seconds, then pause for two minutes. It's exactly like taking the subway, but without the trains.

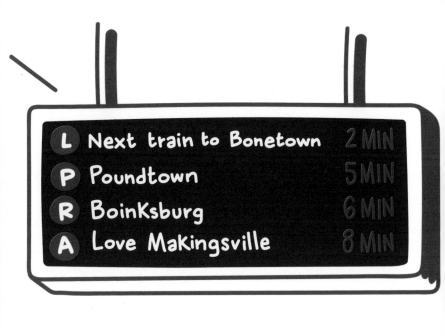

L	Next train to Bonetown	2 MIN
P	Poundtown	5 MIN
R	Boinksburg	6 MIN
A	Love Makingsville	8 MIN

The Scissors

Have sex while holding a pair of scissors so your partner has to be very careful not to cut themselves. This prevents things from getting too out of hand, energy-wise.

The Understudy

When one hole gets tired, best to give another one a shot.

The Bungee

This is risky, but if you really hate voluntary repetitive motion, attach yourself to a bungee cord that hangs from your second-story balcony, stairs, or even a local bridge, then hover over your partner. The bungee will move so you don't have to. Obviously, there's a decent chance you won't land anywhere near their genitals. Also, a decent chance you may die. But hey, absolutely no effort!

JUST THE TIPS

- If you're having sex standing up, wear grippy socks to ensure your feet don't slide. This relieves pressure on your legs.

- Have sex before dinner. No one wants to fuck on a full stomach. Besides, have you ever heard of delayed gratification?

The Unicorn

In this one, invite in a third. Ideally someone who:

1. Is more active than either of you, with better cardiovascular health (for example, someone who is into threesomes and running marathons)

2. Is willing to give head and handies simultaneously

3. Can really take the load off both of you.

JUST THE TIP!

Figure out which of your friends your partner is most attracted to, then keep them on speed dial in case you get tired and need someone to sub in.

The Vibrator

This one is self-explanatory. Outsource all the hard work to your vibrator.

JUST THE TIP!

It can be tempting to buy a battery-powered vibrator so you don't have to deal with charging it. This is discouraged. Studies show you never have any spare batteries when you need them so you have to go out and buy more, but you're definitely not going to do that.

The 69

An iconic sex position for the lazy. You can multitask the oral and then spend the time you saved on watching TV.

The 6

This is like 69, except you don't rotate your body at all, and your partner works around it to service you.

DISCLAIMER: One person actually has to do work here. But it doesn't have to be you.

The Eternal Wheelbarrow

If there's a penis involved in the sex, the penetration itself can be something of a hassle. Best to only do it once, then stay permanently inserted for the remainder of your sexual relationship. You'll figure out how to walk around; it'll be great.

Getting Head

We cannot recommend this enough. Very little effort required on your part.

The Lampshade

Put a lampshade over your head (could be kinky maybe?) so your partner can't see that your eyes are closed and that you are perhaps approaching sleep.

JUST THE TIP!

A mixing bowl works too if you're short on lampshades. You're way too lazy to bake, so you may as well get some use out of it.

The Easy Button

Even the best sex can sometimes involve too much chatting, like when you have to ask your partner if they like that, yeah, right there, like that. In this pose you simply push a button to indicate you've finished, saving both of you your throat muscles. You can even add in more buttons—one for when you want to slow down, one for when you need a break, and one for when you want to go faster (although you probably won't need this one).

The Meryl Streep

Watch anything with Meryl Streep in it—she's good in everything. Her commitment to excellence will remind you to only do things if you're willing to give them 100 percent.

The Debutante

Have sex while balancing a bowl of oranges on your head. Explain that the point is to improve your posture; leave out the fact that the only way this works is if your partner calmly does hand stuff while you do nothing.

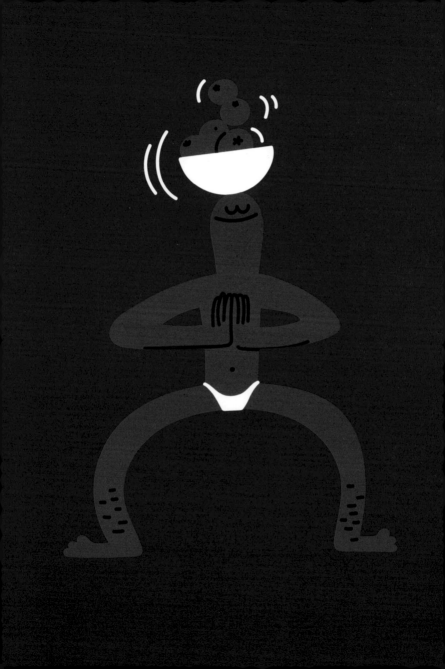

The Pinkie and the Brain

Use only your pinkie finger to get your partner off. Now that is some good thinking.

The Vampire

Lie on your back and keep both arms by your sides like you're in a coffin. There aren't a whole lot of positions available to you—mostly oral sex, or very compact missionary—but at least your arms won't tire out.

JUST THE TIP!

Never volunteer to switch positions—it's too big of a risk. What if you get into the new position and it requires more work? Then everything has backfired. Wait until it's absolutely necessary.

The Treasure Hunt

Plant something in one of your partner's holes, then dig it out. You're giving them sexual pleasure in a task-oriented way, which makes it easier to focus.

DISCLAIMER: Choose your object wisely. Whatever goes in must come out.

The Dumbwaiter

One of you sits on a bed. The other sits inside a dumbwaiter and gets lifted toward the other person's genitalia. Of course, the device itself is expensive, but it's ultimately worth it. The alternative is expending effort—yuck.

JUST THE TIPS

- Get a mattress with extra-bouncy springs to aid in humping your partner—leverage is key. If even this is too much work, simply have sex on a trampoline.

- Quit your job. I've always thought it unfair that people have to find time for both work and sex, you know?

The Incentive Structure

Make a promise to youself: For every minute of effort you get a treat, like buying one of the thousands of items you have saved in your online cart.

The Mimosa

The process of taking off all your clothes is exhausting. Only take off your underwear and pants in this one. Like a mimosa brunch, you're going bottomless.

JUST THE TIP!

It's not fair that boxers and briefs have a convenient hole for genitals. Everyone deserves easy access. If you have underwear that requires removal prior to sex, simply cut a hole in it, saving you the trouble of pushing it over your bum.

The Remote Control

Have sex on top of a remote control so at least you can keep channel surfing. If you're going to bone, you may as well catch up on your shows at the same time.

The Coach

Hire someone to motivate you. Find a coach who can yell things like, "KEEP GOING COME ON YOU CAN DO IT LET'S GO LET'S GO LET'S GO!" during the session. If you find someone with the right kink, you probably won't even need to pay them.

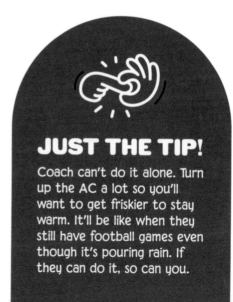

JUST THE TIP!

Coach can't do it alone. Turn up the AC a lot so you'll want to get friskier to stay warm. It'll be like when they still have football games even though it's pouring rain. If they can do it, so can you.

The Bonsai Tree

Having sex while standing is hard. One of you has to lift up a bit and sort of bend over, the other has to squat, and there's a lot of holding each other up, and just—no thanks. Instead, dig a thigh-high hole in the dirt and essentially plant yourself into it. Then, your partner can get it in and you both still enjoy the thrill of standing sex while you get to exert at least 80 percent less energy. Why is it a bonsai and not a real tree? Because you aren't as big as a real tree, obviously! Don't be ridiculous.

The Bondage

Under the guise of kink, let your partner tie your hands to the bed and suggest they do your legs too. This way, not only is moving during sex not an obligation—it's not an option.

JUST THE TIPS

- Avoid clothes with buttons at all costs. It is highly recommended that you invest in tear-away pants.

- If you find yourself on top, put your phone out of reach and have a friend text you every minute. Reaching over to check the notification will cause a little forward momentum—and that's enough work, right?

The Fourway

Bring in two others to have sex with you—you pick one, your partner picks the other. Then, watch those two people have sex. Don't forget the popcorn!

The Diet

If you're giving head, only give a few licks. Claim that you're exercising portion control.

The Chubby Bunny

Diet's over. This time, stuff your mouth full of marshmallows before sex. You can have any kind of intercourse, but you have a good excuse to get out of being the one to do the oral.

The Groundhog

If it's dark outside, take another six weeks off giving oral. By no means does this imply you won't be able to receive oral—plenty of people don't even believe in Groundhog Day.

The Missionary

Except unlike in the traditional missionary position, in this one you role-play devout missionaries who actually aren't allowed to have sex.

The Sex Dream

The laziest sex of all—the kind you have while you're asleep.